THE CLIMATE CRISIS IN HAWAII AND US ISLAND TERRITORIES

by Mary Bates

WWW.FOCUSREADERS.COM

Copyright © 2024 by Focus Readers®, Lake Elmo, MN 55042. All rights reserved. No part of this book may be reproduced or utilized in any form or by any means without written permission from the publisher.

Focus Readers is distributed by North Star Editions:
sales@northstareditions.com | 888-417-0195

Produced for Focus Readers by Red Line Editorial.

Content Consultant: Laura Brewington, PhD, Research Professor at the Global Institute of Sustainability and Innovation, Arizona State University; Research Fellow at the East-West Center

Photographs ©: Shutterstock Images, cover, 1, 8–9, 22–23, 29; Linda Rodriguez Flecha/AP Images, 4–5; Carlos Giusti/AP Images, 7; Red Line Editorial, 10; Matthew S. Masaschi/Planetpix/Alamy, 12; Petty Officer 1st Class Stacy Laseter/Commander Task Force 75/US Navy/DVIDS, 14–15; David Burdick/NOAA, 17; Gerald Lopez Cepero/GDA Photo/AP Images, 18; Jennifer Sinco Kelleher/AP Images, 21; National Park of America Samoa/National Park Services, 25; Priscila Vargas-Babilonia/St. Petersburg Coastal and Marine Science Center/USGS, 27

Library of Congress Cataloging-in-Publication Data
Library of Congress Cataloging-in-Publication Data is available on the Library of Congress website.

ISBN
978-1-63739-629-2 (hardcover)
978-1-63739-686-5 (paperback)
978-1-63739-794-7 (ebook pdf)
978-1-63739-743-5 (hosted ebook)

Printed in the United States of America
Mankato, MN
082023

ABOUT THE AUTHOR

Mary Bates is a freelance science writer and author. She specializes in writing about the life sciences for curious audiences of all ages. Her work has appeared in numerous print and online publications.

TABLE OF CONTENTS

CHAPTER 1

Hurricane Maria 5

CHAPTER 2

Caribbean and Pacific Climates 9

CHAPTER 3

Islands in the Storm 15

THAT'S AMAZING!

Julian Aguon 20

CHAPTER 4

Adapting to the Crisis 23

Focus on Hawaii and US Island Territories • 30
Glossary • 31
To Learn More • 32
Index • 32

CHAPTER 1

HURRICANE MARIA

In September 2017, Hurricane Maria struck Puerto Rico. Puerto Rico is a US island **territory**. It lies in the Caribbean Sea. Maria was the strongest hurricane to hit the island in 80 years.

Hurricane Maria brought winds of up to 155 miles per hour (249 km/h). The winds uprooted trees and broke windows.

A boy in Puerto Rico looks out at the powerful winds of Hurricane Maria on September 20, 2017.

They ripped roofs off homes. In some areas, 20 inches (51 cm) of rain fell over 48 hours. Landslides and flash flooding blocked most roads.

Approximately 3,000 people lost their lives. The hurricane also destroyed Puerto Rico's power grid. The main island lost electricity. More than three million people live there. People struggled to find clean water and food. They had trouble finding gasoline and medical supplies, too. Some of these challenges continued for years.

Puerto Rico has always dealt with hurricanes. But now, **climate change** is making these storms more common. The storms are also becoming stronger.

Power lines were destroyed in the city of Humacao, Puerto Rico.

The climate crisis is impacting the whole world. But US island states and territories have felt some of the earliest harms. They also face some of the most extreme risks.

CHAPTER 2

CARIBBEAN AND PACIFIC CLIMATES

The United States has lands in the Pacific Ocean and the Caribbean Sea. Hawaii is an island state in the Pacific Ocean. There are also 11 US island territories in the Pacific. People live on three of them. They are American Samoa, Guam, and the Northern Mariana Islands.

Tropical rainforests cover many islands in the Pacific Ocean and the Caribbean, including the Hawaiian island Kaua'i.

Three US island territories are in the Caribbean Sea. People live on two. They are Puerto Rico and the US Virgin Islands.

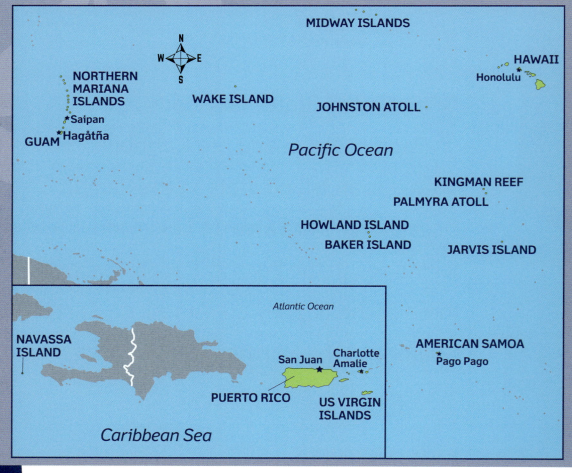

US ISLANDS

The climates of all these islands are similar. They are surrounded by the ocean. Water cools down and warms up more slowly than land does. For this reason, being near the water makes temperatures mild. The islands usually don't have a wide range of temperatures.

Also, these islands are all located in or near the **tropics**. The tropics are closer to the **equator**. They get more sunlight than places farther north or south. This makes the weather warm or hot all year.

In the US island territories, there is typically only a dry season and a wet season. In some areas, the wet season overlaps with hurricane season. This is

A boat in the US Virgin Islands was toppled after Hurricane Irma in 2017.

true for Guam and the Northern Mariana Islands. Hurricane season runs from June through November for most US islands. However, the opposite is true for Hawaii and American Samoa. Their wet seasons run from November through April.

Different parts of these islands receive different amounts of rain. The temperature can also vary. The reason is elevation. That is an area's height compared with sea level. In Puerto Rico, a mountain range divides the north and south parts of the island. The mountains block some of the rain heading south. So, the south is drier. In Hawaii, low elevations tend to be hotter and drier. But its mountain peaks can dip below freezing.

FRESHWATER STREAMS

In Hawaii, freshwater streams flow down from the mountains. The water goes to the plains and then out to sea. The freshwater streams begin within forests in the mountains. For centuries, Native Hawaiians used materials from the forests. They made canoes and fishing nets. They used the fresh water to grow crops in the plains.

CHAPTER 3

ISLANDS IN THE STORM

People burn massive amounts of **fossil fuels**. These fuels provide energy for vehicles, heat, electricity, and more. However, burning fossil fuels releases **greenhouse gases**. These gases enter the atmosphere. Then they absorb energy from the sun. They trap heat near the planet's surface. That is raising Earth's

The US military has bases across the Pacific, including on Guam. The US military is the world's largest single source of greenhouse gases.

average temperatures. It is causing climate change.

This crisis is affecting US islands across the Caribbean Sea and the Pacific Ocean. The oceans are becoming warmer. They are also absorbing more greenhouse gases from the air. This increases **ocean acidity**. These two changes are harming many kinds of ocean life. For example, **coral reefs** have trouble surviving in acidic waters. Many ocean plants and animals depend on coral reefs. People also use resources from the ocean. These include fish and seaweed.

Higher temperatures also lead to other problems. Glaciers are melting.

Higher temperatures and ocean acidity can kill colorful algae in coral reefs. This makes the reefs look white.

As a result, sea levels are rising. Coastal and island areas are especially at risk. Sea level rise is eroding shores. Eroding means wearing away at a surface. It can damage beaches, roads, and buildings.

Climate change is affecting rainfall, too. US islands are receiving less rain overall. Plus, hotter conditions increase **evaporation**. These shifts are reducing freshwater supplies on the islands.

Erosion is clearly visible on a beach in Puerto Rico's capital, San Juan.

At the same time, extreme weather events are happening more often. They are also becoming more intense. These events include storms, hurricanes, floods, droughts, and heat waves.

These changes threaten people and communities. For example, supplies of fresh water and food are at risk. Jobs that rely on natural resources are in danger, too. These include jobs such as fishing and farming. Long-term health dangers are another issue. Floods, hurricanes, and higher temperatures can create conditions that make it easier for diseases to spread.

TERRITORIES AND AID

Climate disasters can cause massive damage. Affected areas often need lots of money and work to recover. The US government helps. It provides money to states and territories after disasters. But territories often receive less money than states. They may also have to wait longer for help because they are so far away. These problems make it much harder to recover from extreme weather events.

THAT'S AMAZING!

JULIAN AGUON

People have lived on Guam for thousands of years. The Chamorro were the first people to make their home there. But in the 1600s, Spanish colonists took over the island. The United States gained control in 1898. Today, the island is a US territory. Residents of Guam are US citizens. But they cannot vote in US national elections.

Guam's legal position gives its residents limited power. These limits can make it difficult to respond to the climate crisis. For this reason, challenging the legal system is one way to fight climate change.

Julian Aguon is a Chamorro lawyer, activist, and writer. He was born on Guam. Aguon started his own law firm when he was 28. As a lawyer, he fights for Indigenous peoples' rights. Indigenous people, such as the Chamorro, have ancestors

Julian Aguon's legal work often focuses on Indigenous peoples' ability to make choices for themselves.

who lived in a region before colonists arrived. Part of Aguon's work for Indigenous rights is protecting the natural environment. He works on Guam and around the Pacific Islands region.

CHAPTER 4

ADAPTING TO THE CRISIS

To help slow climate change, people must use less fossil fuels. Instead, people can use energy such as solar and wind power. Wind power uses turbines. These machines turn when wind hits them. The rotation makes electricity. Solar power uses solar panels. Sunlight hits the panels. Then they produce

Honolulu, the capital of Hawaii, leads US cities in using solar power.

electricity. Renewable energy releases far less greenhouse gases than fossil fuels.

However, the climate crisis is already happening. US island states and territories must adapt to these changes. People also need to prepare for future risks. US island communities are leading the world in these efforts.

Many climate adaptation projects use traditional and Indigenous knowledge. Pacific communities are bringing back traditional farming practices. People are growing crops that can survive droughts. They are using seaweed to add nutrients to the soil. They are planting trees to give their crops shade.

On American Samoa, taro is a key crop. Scientists are working on developing taro that can survive saltier water.

People are also combining traditional practices with new technology. Scientists are developing new crops. These plants can survive hotter temperatures. They can withstand the impacts of rising sea levels. As sea levels rise, ocean water is flooding bodies of fresh water.

25

Ocean water is salty. Many crops cannot survive salt water. But scientists are developing plants that can.

In Puerto Rico, scientists are working with communities. Together, they are bringing back sand dunes along the coasts. These dunes protect against winds, waves, and rising sea levels. They help keep people, the environment, and cultural sites safe. But hurricanes and strong storms have damaged the dunes. The project will help scientists learn why some dunes are more affected by storm damage than other dunes. Then local leaders can identify the best areas of the coast to restore.

One method to restore dunes uses wooden planks. These planks act like native plants that trap sand.

Local governments are also hard at work. In Hawaii, leaders are preparing for shortages of fresh water. They are creating water conservation programs. They are planning for drought.

Other Pacific island governments are collecting food and water resources. This is to prepare for ocean flooding.

People in US island states and territories need help. They want other countries to fight climate change.

MANGROVES

Mangrove trees grow in the salty waters along tropical coastlines. The trees support local communities. Mangroves provide people with food and building materials. They also protect coasts from extreme weather events such as hurricanes. Mangroves defend against powerful winds and waves. Mangroves are also some of the best carbon sinks. Carbon sinks remove and store carbon from the atmosphere. That helps fight climate change.

Mangroves are native and helpful in much of the Pacific but not in Hawaii. There, they are introduced and harmful.

They want world leaders to support clean energy. The whole world must work together to reduce greenhouse gas emissions. Everyone must use more renewable energy options. Islands in the Caribbean and Pacific are showing how to adapt to a changing climate.

FOCUS ON
HAWAII AND US ISLAND TERRITORIES

Write your answers on a separate piece of paper.

1. Write a paragraph describing the main ideas of Chapter 3.

2. What effect of the climate crisis do you think is hardest for islands to adapt to? Why?

3. Where was Julian Aguon born?

> **A.** Hawaii
> **B.** Puerto Rico
> **C.** Guam

4. What would happen if coastal sand dunes were damaged or destroyed?

> **A.** Strong storms would happen more often.
> **B.** Strong storms would cause more harm.
> **C.** Strong storms would be prevented.

Answer key on page 32.

GLOSSARY

climate change
A human-caused global crisis involving long-term changes in Earth's temperature and weather patterns.

coral reefs
Systems of animals that live in warm, shallow waters.

equator
An imaginary line that runs around the middle of Earth.

evaporation
When liquid water turns to water vapor.

fossil fuels
Energy sources that come from the remains of plants and animals that died long ago.

greenhouse gases
Gases that trap heat in Earth's atmosphere.

ocean acidity
A human-caused change in the chemical properties of ocean water, weakening coral skeletons and animal shells.

territory
An area of land that is not a state but is still part of the United States.

tropics
The areas of Earth near the equator.

TO LEARN MORE

BOOKS

Bright, Annie. *Hawaii*. Minneapolis: Abdo Publishing, 2023.

Kington, Emily. *Climate Change*. Truro, UK: Hungry Tomato, 2022.

Thacher, Meg. *Using Solar Farms to Fight Climate Change*. Lake Elmo, MN: Focus Readers, 2023.

NOTE TO EDUCATORS

Visit **www.focusreaders.com** to find lesson plans, activities, links, and other resources related to this title.

INDEX

Aguon, Julian, 20–21
American Samoa, 9–10, 12

Caribbean Sea, 5, 9–10, 16, 29
Chamorro, 20

droughts, 18, 24, 27

fossil fuels, 15, 23–24
fresh water, 13, 17–18, 25, 27

Guam, 9–10, 12, 20–21

Hawaii, 9–10, 12–13, 27
Hurricane Maria, 5–6
hurricanes, 5–6, 11–12, 18–19, 26, 28

Northern Mariana Islands, 9–10, 12

ocean acidity, 16

Pacific Ocean, 9–10, 16, 21, 24, 28–29
Puerto Rico, 5–6, 10, 13, 26

sea level rise, 17, 25–26

US Virgin Islands, 10

Answer Key: **1.** Answers will vary; **2.** Answers will vary; **3.** C; **4.** B